# BOOK-A-TIVITIES!

## High-Interest Activities To Turn Students Into Booklovers

Written and Illustrated by Jan Grubb Philpot

Incentive Publications, Inc.
Nashville, Tennessee

## Dedicated to MY MOST MEMORABLE TEACHERS...

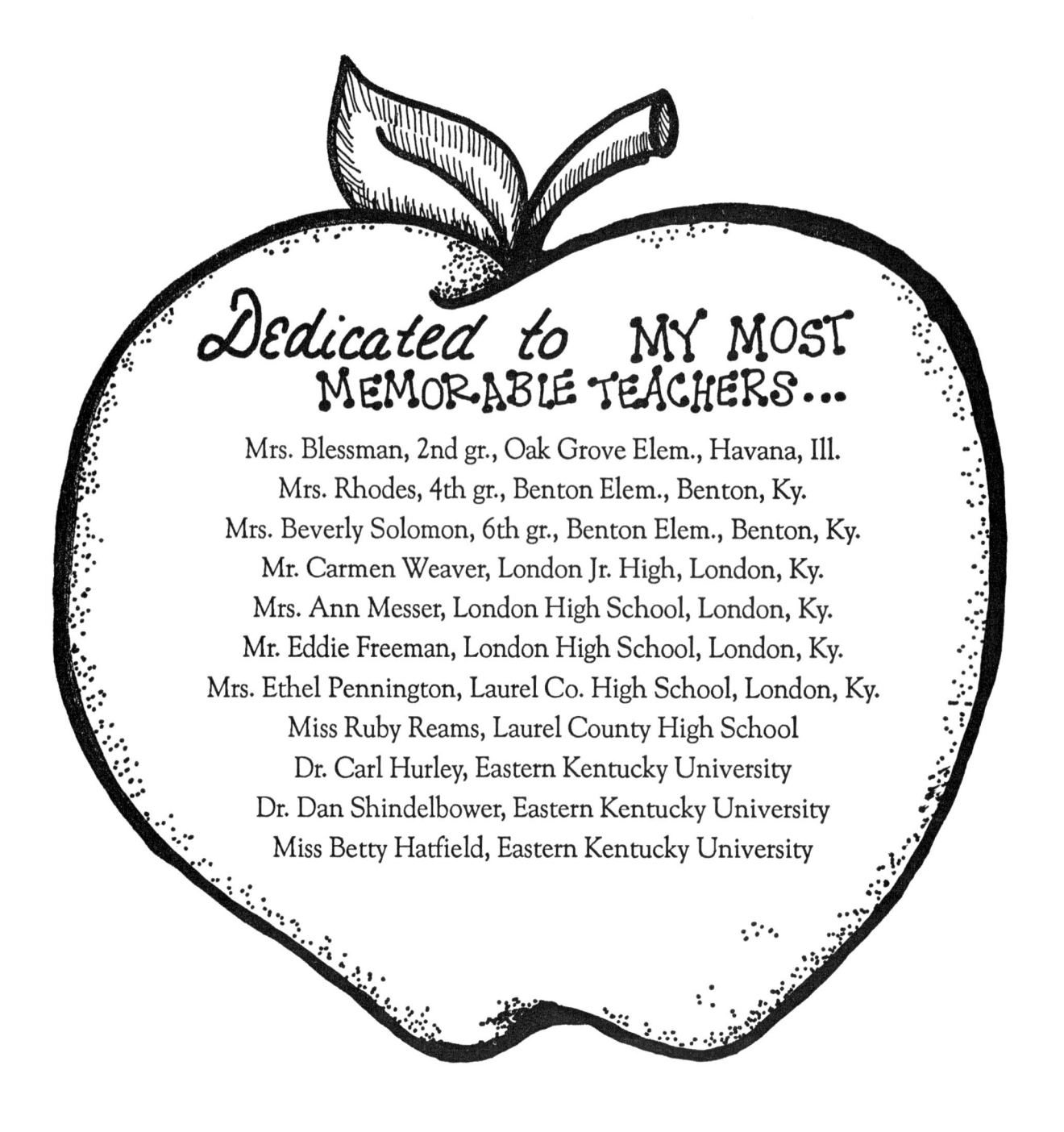

Mrs. Blessman, 2nd gr., Oak Grove Elem., Havana, Ill.
Mrs. Rhodes, 4th gr., Benton Elem., Benton, Ky.
Mrs. Beverly Solomon, 6th gr., Benton Elem., Benton, Ky.
Mr. Carmen Weaver, London Jr. High, London, Ky.
Mrs. Ann Messer, London High School, London, Ky.
Mr. Eddie Freeman, London High School, London, Ky.
Mrs. Ethel Pennington, Laurel Co. High School, London, Ky.
Miss Ruby Reams, Laurel County High School
Dr. Carl Hurley, Eastern Kentucky University
Dr. Dan Shindelbower, Eastern Kentucky University
Miss Betty Hatfield, Eastern Kentucky University

*Cover by Jan Grubb Philpot*
*Edited by Jan Keeling*

ISBN 0-86530-248-0

Copyright © 1993 by Incentive Publications, Inc., Nashville, TN. All rights reserved. No part of this publication may be reproduced, stored in a retrieval system, or transmitted in any form or by any means (electronic, mechanical, photocopying, recording, or otherwise) without written permission from Incentive Publications, Inc., with the exception below.

Pages labeled with the statement © 1993 by Incentive Publications, Inc., Nashville, TN are intended for reproduction. Permission is hereby granted to the purchaser of one copy of BOOK-A-TIVITIES! to reproduce these pages in sufficient quantities for meeting the purchaser's own classroom needs.

# Table of Contents

Preface .................................................................................................6

**IT'S ANYBODY'S GUESS** (*A Collection of Quiz Activities Designed to Lure Children into Books!*)
- What's My Line? (*Primary Activity*) ...........................................................8
- What's My Line? (*Student Worksheet*) .........................................................9
- Name That Character! (*Primary Activity*) ...................................................15
- Who Dun It? (*Intermediate Activity*) .........................................................17
- Who Dun It? (*Student Worksheet*) ............................................................18
- Lost . . . and Found? (*Primary Activity*) ...................................................21
- Books Make Headlines! (*Primary or Intermediate Activity*) ..........................28
- Be A Star Reporter! (*Student Worksheet*) ...................................................30
- Hats Off To Characters! (*Primary Activity*) ...............................................32
- Hats Off To Characters! (*Student Worksheets*) .......................................33-34

**BOOK BAIT!** (*Classroom Activities, Programs, and Displays Designed to "Hook 'Em On Reading!"*)
- Book Graffiti Wall.................................................................................36
- A Reading Genealogy.............................................................................37
- A Reading Genealogy (*Student Worksheets*) .........................................39-40
- A Reader's Time Capsule........................................................................42
- Break For The Books Day!......................................................................44
- The Book Buck Incentive!.......................................................................51
- Knock, Knock! On My Door!..................................................................54

**GAMES READERS PLAY**
- The Name Game....................................................................................60
- I'm A Bookworm...................................................................................61
- Shake Out The Characters!.....................................................................62
- Storybook Beano!..................................................................................64

In our bustling modern age, children may be as busy as adults, hurrying to ballgames, music lessons, school activities, etc. Often there is not much time left for leisure reading. If we want students to discover books—we've got to provide the bait! This book is not about making book reports or reading with a critical eye. This book is intended to make the IDEA of reading so much fun that students won't realize what's happened until they discover they have become true booklovers! *Book-A-Tivities!*, which may be used as a companion to *Book-A-Brations* (Incentive Publications, 1990), is a serendipitous collection of book-search activities, scavenger hunts, games, and classroom correlations, all designed to entice students to discover quality children's literature. It is intended for classroom teachers, librarians, reading teachers, and parents. All activities are the any-time drop-of-a-hat kind, complete with instructions, masters, patterns, and awards for quick and easy classroom use.

*Happy Reading!*

# IT'S ANYBODY'S GUESS

A COLLECTION OF QUIZ ACTIVITIES DESIGNED TO *Lure Children Into Books!*

# WHAT'S MY LINE?

"What's My Line?" is an activity that will have primary children carefully examining illustrations in picture books for answers to a puzzling dilemma. Fifteen items of character apparel are provided; students are to discover the character associated with each item.

## PLANNING SUGGESTIONS

1. Duplicate the items of apparel on pages 10-13. You may choose to enlarge these, using an opaque projector or a duplicating machine. Color and laminate, then use clothespins to attach to a clothesline strung in your classroom.

2. Explain to students that they are to help return the "laundry" to the appropriate owners. You will need to pull the appropriate books from the library and display them in your classroom.

   Give each student (or group) a copy of the answer sheet on page 9. Tell them they do not have to work in any particular order. This activity works best when done with groups or as a spare-time individual activity.

3. Each student or group who completes the puzzle receives an award (page 14).

*Note:* If you do not choose to display the specific books from which you want answers chosen, you will need to be somewhat flexible when judging the answers—other picturebook characters may wear similar apparel.

©1993 by Incentive Publications, Inc., Nashville, TN.

# WHAT'S MY LINE?

Don't let this activity "wash you up"! Fifteen characters need their laundry returned! Examine books in the display and return each item to its rightful owner. Be sure to match the number of the clothing hanging on the line with the numbered line below!

1. _____
2. _____
3. _____
4. _____
5. _____
6. _____
7. _____
8. _____
9. _____
10. _____
11. _____
12. _____
13. _____
14. _____
15. _____

Name(s) _____

©1993 by Incentive Publications, Inc., Nashville, TN.

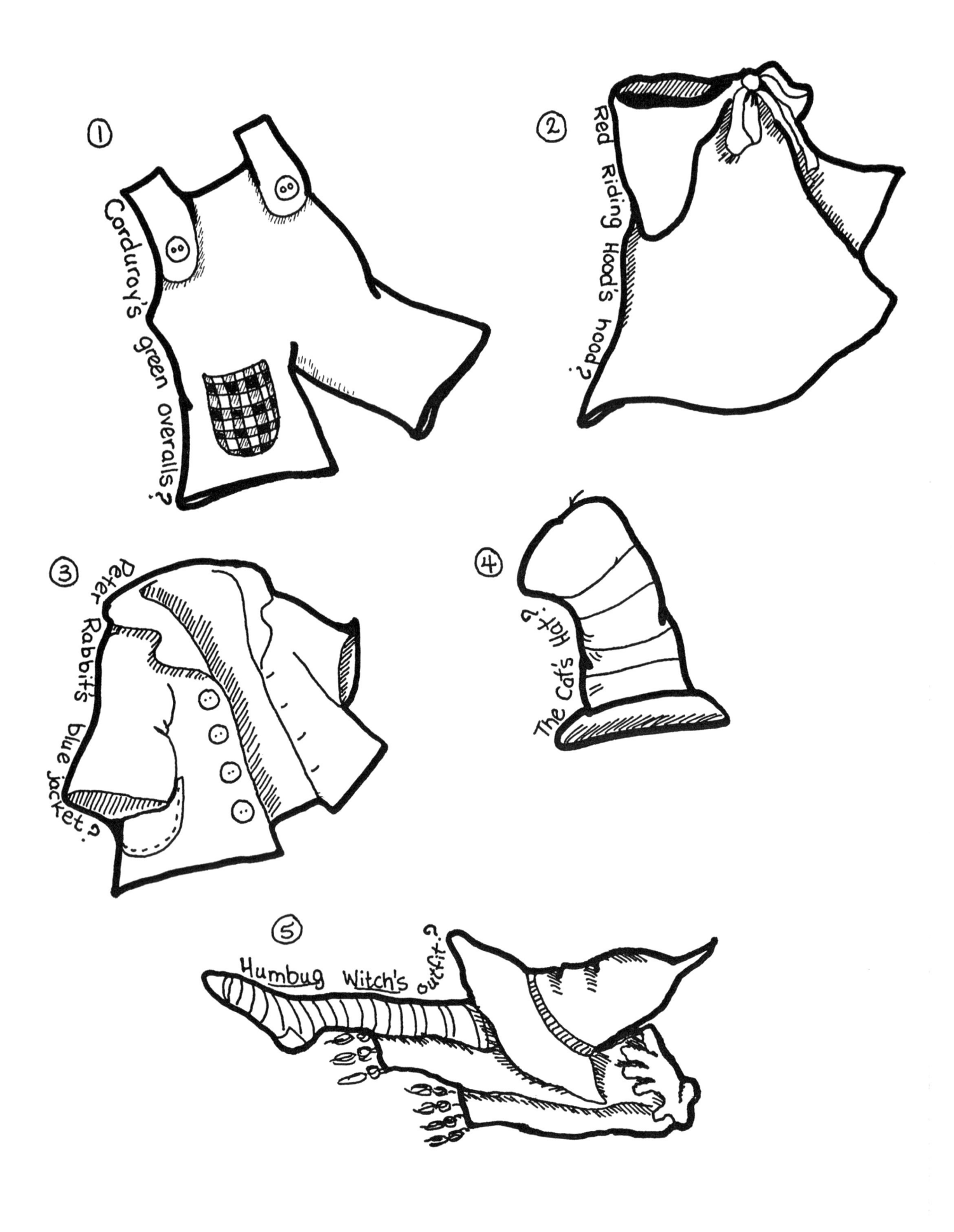

1. Corduroy's green overalls?
2. Red Riding Hood's hood?
3. Peter Rabbit's blue jacket?
4. The Cat's hat?
5. Humbug Witch's outfit?

6. Amelia Bedelia's maid uniform?

7. The "Madeline look"?

8. The "Man with the yellow hat's" style?

©1993 by Incentive Publications, Inc., Nashville, TN.

9. Remember Mike Mulligan?

10. A frog suit?

11. Duds for a tin man?...

©1993 by Incentive Publications, Inc., Nashville, TN.

12

12. Appropriate apparel for a tin soldier?

13. A wolf suit for Max the King?

14. Peter Pan flies in style?

15. Je suis Anatole?

©1993 by Incentive Publications, Inc., Nashville, TN.

attach your photograph here!

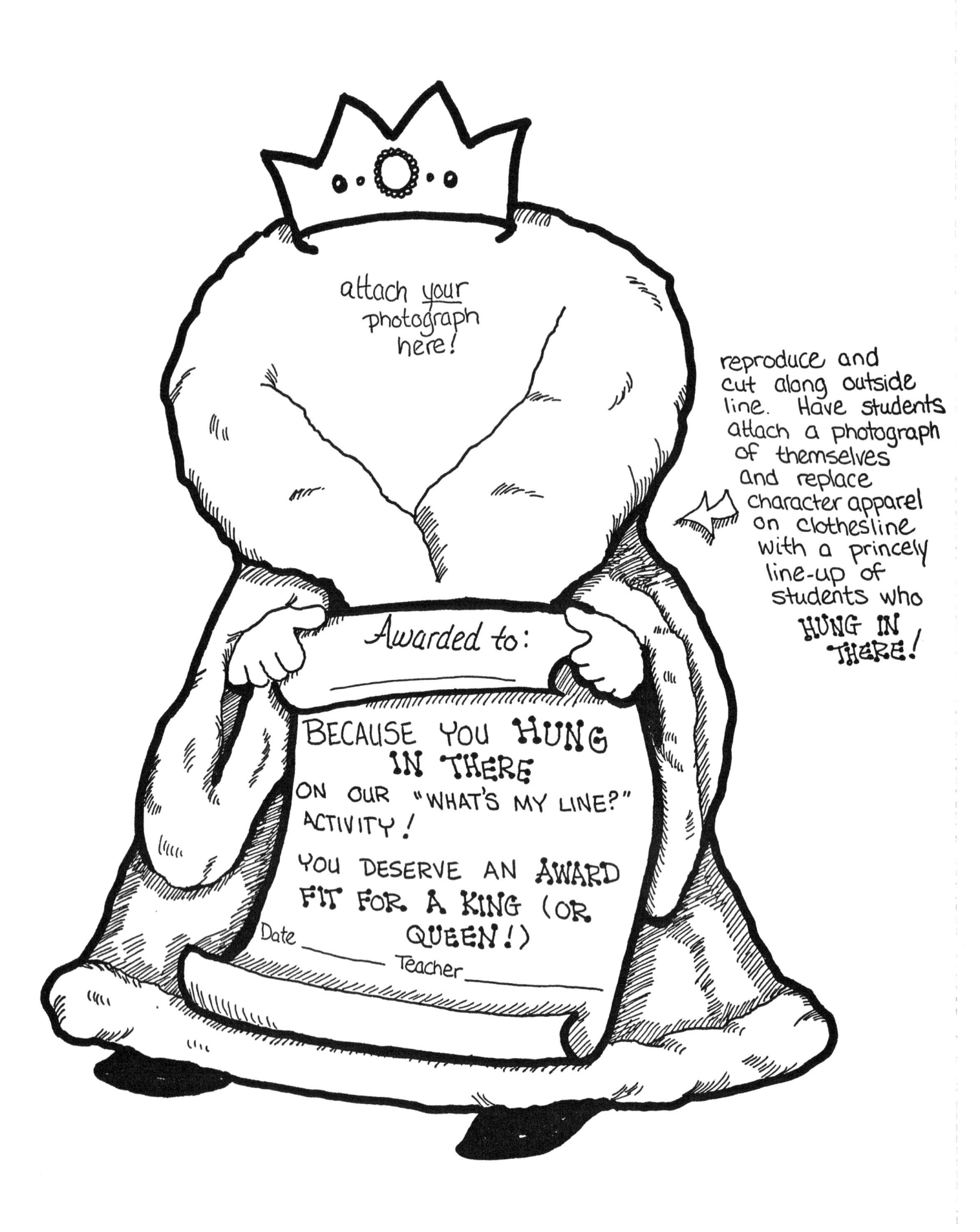

Awarded to: _____

BECAUSE YOU HUNG IN THERE ON OUR "WHAT'S MY LINE?" ACTIVITY!

YOU DESERVE AN AWARD FIT FOR A KING (OR QUEEN!)

Date _____ Teacher _____

reproduce and cut along outside line. Have students attach a photograph of themselves and replace character apparel on clothesline with a princely line-up of students who HUNG IN THERE!

©1993 by Incentive Publications, Inc., Nashville, TN.

# NAME THAT CHARACTER!

"Name That Character!" is a good way to put all those old book catalogs and advertisements to good use, as you send children scurrying to library shelves for answers! Here's how:

   1. Clip illustrations of favorite book characters from catalogs, advertisements, and old book jackets. (Hint: if you don't have an abundance of these, ask your librarian. She's sure to have some!) Some of the characters that are easy to locate are: Curious George, Corduroy, Amelia Bedelia, Arthur, the Cat in the Hat, the Grinch, a "Wild Thing," and Miss Viola Swamp.

   2. Mount the illustrations on a bulletin board and number them.

NAME THAT CHARACTER!
*page 2*

3. Have students number a sheet of paper and write in the correct character's name. Make this activity last at least a week—students can use their spare time to search the library for characters they don't recognize.

4. Award a special prize for those students who identify all the characters. (You may choose to use the award below). Or let students choose a character from the display. Laminate the chosen characters for students to use as bookmarks.

for _____:
SO GLAD YOU WERE ABLE TO
PIN A NAME
on all those characters in our "Name that Character" activity!

Date _____  Teacher _____

©1993 by Incentive Publications, Inc., Nashville, TN.

# Who Dun It?

Here's a quiz activity that will get students diving into books and looking *beyond* the illustrations for answers! Who knows? During the course of flipping through pages to discover "who done it," a student may become so interested in a case that he or she won't be able to put the book down!

## HERE'S HOW IT WORKS:

1. Motivate the students with the idea of being book "detectives." Give them a special "identification card."

2. Duplicate copies of their case load, "Who Dun It?: A Quiz for Book Detectives" (page 18). Hand these out and tell the students to report back to the Chief of Investigations (yourself!).

3. Give students plenty of time to browse through the books, investigating thoroughly. You might make this a spare-time activity or a creative homework assignment for a long weekend (get those students acquainted with the public library!), or schedule a special research period with your school librarian. You can make this an individual activity or divide the class into detective "squads."

4. Reward the first person or team to locate the missing characters with the "Commendation" on page 20, or use the "Book Buck" idea on page 53.

*Make it official!*

> This certifies that _____ is an official *Book Detective* operating under-covers of good books!
>
> _____ Chief of Investigations

17

# Who Dun It?

1. Who shot *Old Yeller?* _____
2. Who cut off the fox's tail on *One Fine Day?* _____
3. Who cheated Andrew with a recipe for *Freckle Juice?* _____
4. Who told *Harriet the Spy* it was okay to lie? _____
5. Who sneaked and used *Strega Nona's* pasta pot? _____
6. Who captured *The Funny Little Woman?* _____
7. Knowing *Leprechauns Never Lie*, who kidnapped and tried to blackmail a leprechaun? _____
8. Who was really at fault for the death of an owlet in *Why Mosquitoes Buzz in People's Ears?* _____
9. Which *Mother Goose* character stole a pig? _____
10. Which two boys disobeyed their mother and played near a well in *Tikki Tikki Tembo?* _____
11. Which *Mother Goose* character cut off the tails of some blind mice? _____
12. Who smoked cigars in the church restroom during practice for *The Best Christmas Pageant Ever?* _____
13. Who attacked J. T. because of a stolen transistor radio? _____
14. Who punched Nick for calling him a "crybaby" in *Alexander and the Terrible, Horrible, No Good, Very Bad Day?* _____
15. Who tells fibs to and about Cybil in *Cybil's War?* _____
16. Who tracks down a pair of turkey thieves in *Philip Hall Likes Me. I Reckon Maybe?* _____
17. Who makes mischief of one kind and another and has to go live *Where The Wild Things Are?* _____
18. Who bets Billy $50 that he doesn't know *How To Eat Fried Worms?* _____
19. Who did not really want to follow the rules of *Jumanji*, until she realized she'd *better?* _____
20. Who stole the peddler's *Caps for Sale?* _____
21. Who wants to throw away Aunt Dew's *Hundred Penny Box?* _____
22. In the *500 Hats of Bartholomew Cubbins*, who threatens to execute Bartholomew if he does not remove his hats? _____
23. Who was a threat to the *Three Billy Goats Gruff?* _____
24. Patrick has a missing *Aminal!* Track it down and find out what it was and where it was. _____
25. Who were Norwegian children able to slip a *Snow Treasure* past on their sleds? _____

Name(s) _____

© 1993 by Incentive Publications, Inc., Nashville, TN.

# Who Dun It?
## *Answer Page*

1. Travis. *Old Yeller*, Fred Gipson. Harper and Row.
2. The Old Woman. *One Fine Day*, Nonnie Hogrogrian. MacMillan.
3. Sharon. *Freckle Juice*, Judy Blume. Dutton.
4. Old Golly. *Harriet the Spy*, Louise Fitzhugh. Dell.
5. Big Anthony. *Strega Nona*, Tomie de Paola. Prentice Hall.
6. The wicked Oni. *The Funny Little Woman*, Arlene Mosel. Dutton.
7. Ninny Nanny. *Leprechauns Never Lie*, Lorna Balian. Abingdon.
8. The mosquito. *Why Mosquitoes Buzz in People's Ears*, Verna Aardema. Dial.
9. Tom, the piper's son. *Mother Goose*.
10. Chang and Tikki Tikki Tembo-No Sa Rembo-Chari Bari Ruchi-Pip Peri Pembo. *Tikki Tikki Tembo*, Arlene Mosel. SBS.
11. The farmer's wife. *Mother Goose*.
12. Imogene. *The Best Christmas Pageant Ever*, Barbara Robinson. Harper and Row.
13. Claymore and Boomer. *J.T.*, Jane Wagner. Dell.
14. Alexander. *Alexander and the Terrible, Horrible, No Good, Very Bad Day*, Judith Viorst. Atheneum.
15. Tony. *Cybil War*, Betsy Byars. Viking.
16. Beth. *Philip Hall Likes Me. I Reckon Maybe*, Bette Greene. Dial.
17. Max. *Where the Wild Things Are*, Maurice Sendak. Harper and Row.
18. Alan. *How to Eat Fried Worms*, Thomas Rockwell. Watts.
19. Judy and Peter. *Jumanji*, Chris Van Allsburg. Houghton Mifflin.
20. Monkeys. *Caps for Sale*, Esphyr Slobodkina. Harper and Row.
21. Michael's mother. *The Hundred-Penny Box*, Sharon Mathis. Viking.
22. The king. *The 500 Hats of Bartholomew Cubbins*, Dr. Seuss. Vanguard.
23. The troll. *Three Billy Goats Gruff*, Paul Galdone. Houghton Mifflin.
24. A turtle, under the porch. *The Aminal*, Lorna Balian. Abingdon.
25. The Nazis. *The Snow Treasure*, Marie McSwiggan. SBS.

# SPECIAL COMMENDATION

to _____

for tracking down answers in our "WHO DUN IT?" activity!

Date _____  Character _____

REWARD THOSE "BOOK DETECTIVES"!

BOOKS I DISCOVERED ALONG WITH "WHO DUN IT?"!

⇐ A BOOKMARKER FOR KEEPING TRACK OF BOOKS STUDENTS WANT TO "INVESTIGATE FURTHER"!

# LOST... AND FOUND?

"Lost and Found" revolves around a theme of losses of characters in stories. It is a great way to get students inspecting books for answers... and, perhaps, to get them "hooked" in the process! In the clues provided for you, picture books and timeless classics are used as examples, but feel free to use your own ideas to extend this activity and accommodate students past third grade.

## PLANNING SUGGESTIONS

1. Set up your "Lost and Found" display. Reproduce or enlarge the items found on pages 23-26. Another way to do this activity is to create a display using *real* objects. Be sure to number each item.

2. Announce to students that book characters have lost these items and you need help returning them to their rightful owners. Ask each student to write the numbers 1 to 15 on a piece of paper. This list will be used when keeping track of characters to whom objects will be returned. This may be an individual or a team activity.

If you feel the students of your grade level will be unable to locate answers simply by visiting the library, limit their choices and make the task more manageable by creating a display of the books involved.

# LOST... AND FOUND?
## page 2

For non-readers and beginning readers, simply make the display and explain that you will be reading books aloud and sharing books through audiovisual means. Explain that they must keep their ears open and their thinking caps on in order to label a character match-up on the display. This should be treated as a class activity rather than as a competitive quiz.

3. Give a "Terrific Finder Award" (page 27) to each individual or team (or to the class) that discovers all the answers! Smile to yourself, because only YOU know the REAL reward was seeing your students inspecting books they might otherwise never have discovered!

---

### ANSWER KEY TO ITEMS ON PAGES 23-26

1. Lost by Corduroy. *Corduroy*, Freeman.
2. Lost by peddler. *Caps for Sale*, Slobodkina.
3. Lost by the 3 little kittens. *Mother Goose*.
4. Lost by the fox. *One Fine Day*, Hogrogrian.
5. Lost by the Cat in the Hat. *The Cat in the Hat*, Seuss.
6. Lost by Cinderella. *Cinderella*.
7. Lost by mother bear. *Blueberries for Sal*, McCloskey.
8. Lost by Sylvester. *Sylvester and the Magic Pebble*, Steig.
9. Lost by Peter Rabbit. *The Tale of Peter Rabbit*, Potter.
10. Lost by Dorothy. *The Wizard of Oz*, Baum.
11. Lost by Nikki. *The Mitten*, Brett.
12. Lost by children of room 207. *Miss Nelson is Missing*, Allard.
13. Lost by Patrick. *The Aminal*, Balian.
14. Owner: Charlotte. *Charlotte's Web*, White.
15. Lost by Little Bo Peep. *Mother Goose*.

① FOUND in Dept. Store toy section: ONE BUTTON

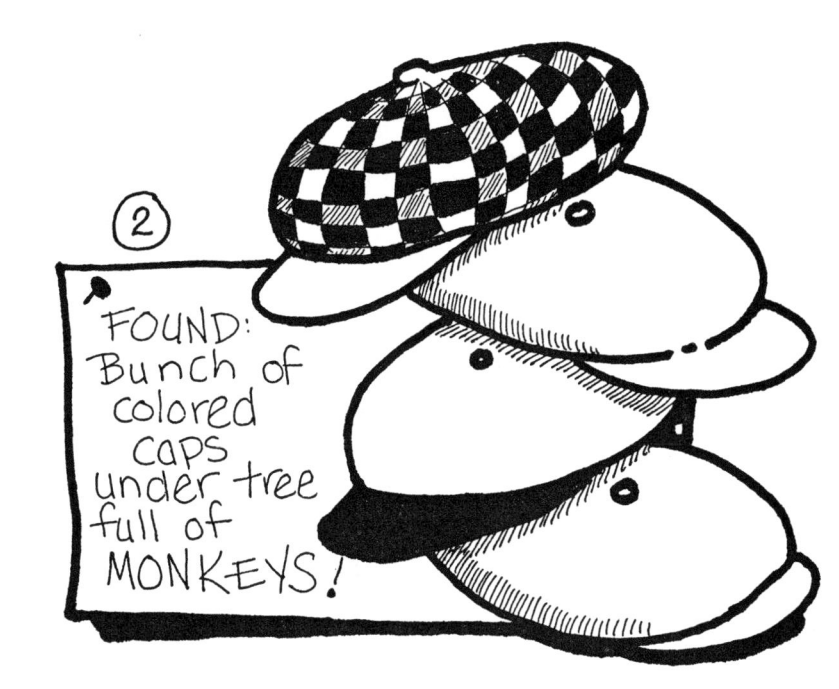

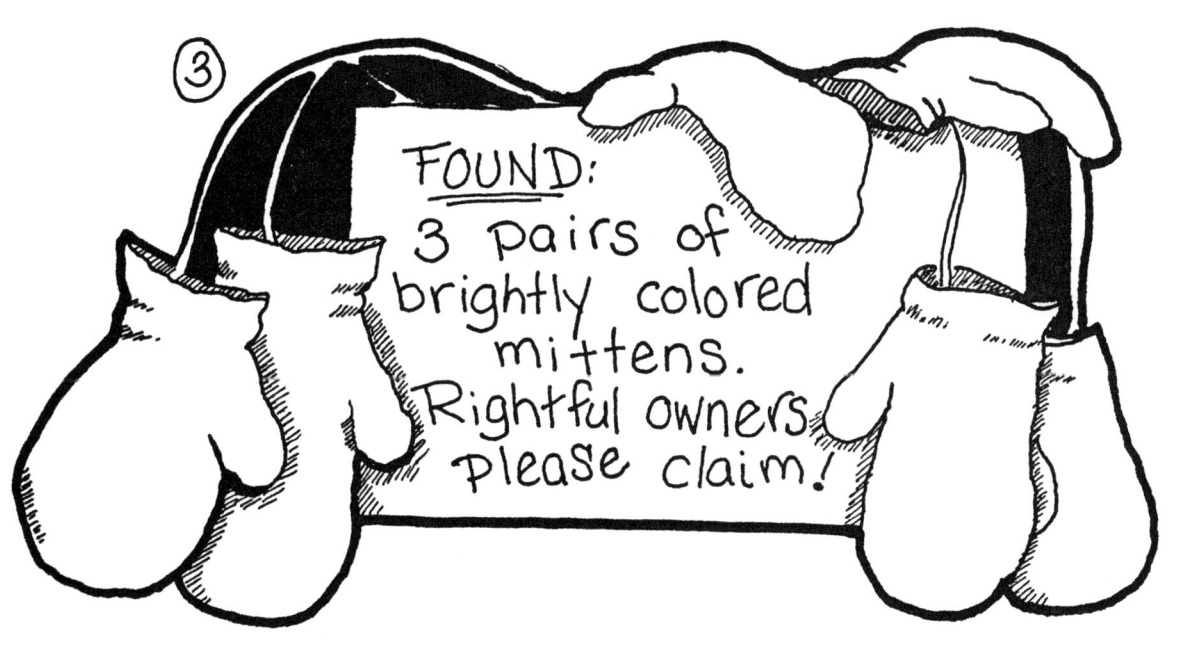

② FOUND: Bunch of colored caps under tree full of MONKEYS!

③ FOUND: 3 pairs of brightly colored mittens. Rightful owners please claim!

④ FOUND: One fox tail! Please claim before your friends laugh at you!

Reproduce same size or enlarge for "Lost and Found" display.

©1993 by Incentive Publications, Inc., Nashville, TN.

⑤ FOUND: one "moss-covered, 3-handled family gredunza." Please CLAIM NOW!

⑥ FOUND: Unusual glass slipper. Must be sadly missed by owner!

⑦ FOUND near Blueberry Hill... One small, lost bear... Rightful owner Please come forward!

©1993 by Incentive Publications, Inc., Nashville, TN.

⑧ FOUND: one red pebble with mystical powers near Strawberry Hill. Please claim!

⑨ FOUND near McGregor Place: blue jacket, gold trim. Initials P.R. in collar.

⑩ Beautiful red slipper located in vicinity of Emerald City...Looking for rightful owner.

⑪ FOUND: One beautiful white knitted mitten. Found in snow near hedgehog, owl, bear and other creatures of forest.

**FOUND!** one real sweet teacher by name of MISS NELSON! Claims children of room _?_ are searching for her! ⑫

**FOUND: one turtle "AMINAL"** under porch! Please claim... May be "ferocious"! ⑬

SOME CLUE

**FOUND!** MIRACLE SPIDER WEB IN WHICH MESSAGES MAGICALLY APPEAR! WILL TALENTED OWNER PLEASE STEP FORWARD? ⑭

**FOUND: one flock of sheep.** Will missing shepherd(ess?) please claim IMMEDIATELY?! ⑮

# Terrific Finder Award

Awarded to _____

for helping locate missing items belonging to book characters!

Date _____   Teacher _____

◀ A REWARD FOR "FINDERS"

Lucky Book Finds

◀ HELP STUDENTS KEEP TRACK OF "LUCKY FINDS" THEY MAKE DURING THE ACTIVITY AND WANT TO RETURN TO AND READ!

©1993 by Incentive Publications, Inc., Nashville, TN.

# EXTRA! EXTRA! READ ALL ABOUT IT!

## BOOKS MAKE HEADLINES!

Another Book-a-tivity that will have students discovering books they might otherwise never pick up is "Books Make Headlines." Here's how to have a successful program:

1. Create a bulletin board display using the little fellow at the top of this page and a number of headlines describing book plots beneath him. (Hint: if you have access to a computer/printer and a computer graphics program, you can create some very authentic-looking headlines). A list of primary book headlines and a list of intermediate book headlines are provided, but have some fun and create some of your OWN headlines!

2. So that identifying the headlines won't be an overwhelming task, pull the books from the library and create a display of books to examine. (You might be just a *little* sneaky and throw in a few for which you have no headlines!)

3. Explain to students that they are to find the book that goes with each headline. Give students an answer sheet (page 30) to fill in as they discover answers. (Hint: explain that this is a spare-time activity and let this activity work as a learning center!)

4. Give all the "star reporters" that discover the answers a Bookitzer Prize Award (page 31), PUT THEIR NAMES in headlines, and display! As a follow-up activity, you might want to have individual students write headlines about books in your classroom collection for classmates to guess!

©1993 by Incentive Publications, Inc., Nashville, TN.

BOOKS MAKE HEADLINES!
page 2

# Primary Book Headlines

- FAMILY OF DUCKS CAUSES TRAFFIC JAM (*Make Way For Ducklings*, McCloskey)
- TWO BROTHERS RESCUED FROM WELL (*Tikki Tikki Tembo*, Mosel)
- MAN DIGS CELLAR, FORGETS TO LEAVE WAY OUT (*Mike Mulligan and His Steam Shovel*, Burton)
- WOMAN KIDNAPPED BY ONI, KEEPS SENSE OF HUMOR (*The Funny Little Woman*, Mosel)
- MISSING DONKEY MYSTERY RESOLVED (*Sylvester and the Magic Pebble*, Steig)
- PARTY RESPONSIBLE FOR DEATH OF OWLET DISCOVERED (*Why Mosquitoes Buzz in People's Ears*, Aardema)
- ELDERLY LADY MAIMS FOX (*One Fine Day*, Hogrogrian)
- GIRL IN COMA AFTER EATING POISONED APPLE (*Snow White*)
- HOUSE SADDENED BY GROWTH OF COMMUNITY (*The Little House*, Burton)
- STRANGE CAT MAKES SHAMBLES OF HOUSE (*The Cat in the Hat*, Seuss)
- WOLF CLAIMS INNOCENCE IN DEATH OF THREE PIGS (*The True Story of the Three Little Pigs*, Scieszka)
- EXCITING NEW DISCOVERY: FRECKLE REMOVER! (*Freckle Juice*, Blume)
- TONS OF PASTA OVERWHELM LOCAL VILLAGE (*Strega Nona*, de Paola)
- MISSING TEACHER CAUSES CONSTERNATION (*Miss Nelson is Missing*, Allard)
- BOY'S GREATEST DESIRE TO VISIT AUSTRALIA (*Alexander and the Terrible, Horrible, No Good, Very Bad Day*, Viorst)

# Intermediate Book Headlines

- MIRACLE SPIDER WEB APPEARS ON FARM (*Charlotte's Web*, White)
- JUVENILE ACCUSED OF SPYING ON FRIENDS AND NEIGHBORS (*Harriet the Spy*, Fitzhugh)
- DONUT MACHINE GOES HAYWIRE (*Homer Price*, McCloskey)
- 14-YEAR-OLD GIRL VOWS TO KEEP FAMILY TOGETHER (*Where the Lilies Bloom*, Cleaver)
- MAN JAILED FOR TRYING TO FEED HUNGRY FAMILY (*Sounder*, Armstrong)
- LOCAL BOY EXISTS ON DIET OF WORMS (*How to Eat Fried Worms*, Rockwell)
- UNUSUAL FAMILY DISCOVERS SECRET OF ETERNAL YOUTH (*Tuck Everlasting*, Babbitt)
- BOY SWALLOWS TURTLE (*Superfudge*, Blume)
- SPIDER FORGES BONDS BETWEEN BOY AND STEPFATHER (*Like Jake and Me*, Jukes)
- GOLDEN TICKET PROVIDES DREAM TRIP (*Charlie and the Chocolate Factory*, Dahl)
- MAIL-ORDER BRIDE ARRIVES (*Sarah, Plain and Tall*, MacLachlan)
- BOY SURVIVES PLANE CRASH, WILDERNESS DANGERS (*Hatchet*, Paulsen)
- LOCAL CHURCH FIRE TURNS OUT TO BE CIGAR SMOKER (*The Best Christmas Pageant Ever*, Robinson)
- GRANDMOTHER WAITS YEARS FOR MESSAGE FROM THE DEAD (*The Eyes of the Amaryllis*, Babbitt)
- LOCAL FAMILY AIDS IN ESCAPE FROM NAZIS (*Number the Stars*, Lowry)

# Be a Star Reporter!

STUDENTS: Examine our Headline Book Display and match the headlines on the bulletin board with books in the display.
Important! Note the number of the headline and write the correct title on the same numbered line below.

1. _____
2. _____
3. _____
4. _____
5. _____
6. _____
7. _____
8. _____
9. _____
10. _____
11. _____
12. _____
13. _____
14. _____
15. _____

©1993 by Incentive Publications, Inc., Nashville, TN.

# The Bookitzer Prize
## for STAR REPORTING!

Awarded for TRACKING DOWN HEADLINES!

awarded to _____

date _____   teacher _____

\* *Note to the teacher:* SO STUDENTS UNDERSTAND THEIR "BOOKITZER PRIZE", NOW IS A GOOD TIME TO INTRODUCE THE PULITZER PRIZE GIVEN IN THE U.S. EACH YEAR FOR OUTSTANDING ACHIEVEMENT IN JOURNALISM... AND LITERATURE... AND DRAMA... AND MUSIC!!!

BOOKS MAKE HEADLINES

HEADLINERS I DON'T WANT TO MISS!

a bookmark to keep track of "headliners" students want to read later!

# HATS OFF to CHARACTERS!

HATS OFF TO CHARACTERS is a primary scavenger hunt that will have students examining illustrations of picture books and classics carefully—and getting "hooked" in the process! This simple activity requires very little preparation, but if you wish to make it even simpler for younger children, display the following books:

>*Peter Pan*, Barrie. Random House.
>*Curious George*, Rey. Houghton Mifflin.
>*Amelia Bedelia*, Parish. Harper and Row.
>*Cinderella*, any version.
>*Strega Nona*, de Paola. Prentice Hall.
>*The Cat in the Hat*, Seuss. Random House.
>*A Bear Called Paddington*, Bond. Dell.
>*Alice in Wonderland*, Carroll, any version.
>*Caps for Sale*, Slobodkina. Harper and Row.
>*Humbug Witch*, Balian. Abingdon.

Reproduce pages 33-34 for students. Allow them to search for the headgear for each character and draw it on their worksheets!

# Hats off to Characters!

If you went to a costume party, what hat would you wear...

If you went as Peter Pan?

If you went as the "man with the yellow hat"?

If you went as Amelia Bedelia?

If you went as Cinderella?

Hint: ILLUSTRATIONS IN BOOKS WILL HELP YOU!

Name(s)

©1993 by Incentive Publications, Inc., Nashville, TN.

If you went as Strega Nona?

If you went as the "Cat in the Hat"?

If you went as Paddington?

If you went as a "Mad Hatter"?

If you had "caps for sale"?

If you decided to be a "Humbug Witch"?

Name(s) _____

# BOOK BAIT!

*LINING UP READERS! by: I.M. Hooked*

Classroom activities, programs, & displays designed to "hook 'em on reading!"

# Book Graffiti Wall

What child wouldn't love to have permission to write on a wall? Children will love this activity, for not only is it "okay" to write on the wall—graffiti is ENCOURAGED! Children's book graffiti will turn "peer pressure" into a positive force for reading motivation!

Of course, there must be rules!
1. All graffiti must remain on the paper attached to the wall.
2. All graffiti must be used to share books students have read.

*Hint:* Contact paper and bulletin board paper are both available in prints that simulate bricks. You may choose to use a brick print for your graffiti wall. If you use contact paper, be sure to furnish a permanent marker for the graffiti!

# A Reading Genealogy

The author of this book remembers discovering *Coppertoed Boots* as a child, followed by such treasures as *The Hundred Dresses* and *The Boxcar Children*. These treasures were discovered when I asked the simple question, "Mom, what was your favorite book when *you* were a little girl?" From these memories came the idea for "A Reading Genealogy."

Use the Reading Genealogy to help your students discover favored reading from other times, very good books that may have been pushed to the "back burner" by the vast amount of books published each year by contemporary publishers. You will discover that many students will find surprising common interests and begin book-sharing with family members! Many teachers have students research family trees as a part of a history lesson—use this Reading Genealogy as a way to bring in the books!

## PLANNING SUGGESTIONS

1. Reproduce "A Reading Genealogy" (page 39) and "More Family Favorites" (page 40) for your students. Give your students several days to interview family members. Encourage the students to write to relatives in other areas of the country for answers. You might tie this in with a lesson on letter writing.

2. Display the completed genealogies so that students can compare the results of their surveys. When the same title crops up again and again, you can be sure it is a classic!

# A READING GENEALOGY
*page 2*

3. Reproduce the Family Favorites Reading Record (page 41) for students to complete. Encourage them to read the books their aunts, uncles, parents, and grandparents enjoyed as children.

4. Give an award to each child who completes the Reading Genealogy and discovers new old books.

## ADDITIONAL IDEAS FOR A SUCCESSFUL PROGRAM

- Read the class the book that was YOUR favorite as a child.

- Invite parents and grandparents into the classroom to read favorite selections to the class.

- Remind the students that children of today have a way of becoming the parents and grandparents of tomorrow and the books so popular with them today may not always be popular. Help the students create a "Time Capsule" containing favorite titles. Arrange for the "Time Capsule" to be stored in the school library and opened by young readers in 10 or 20 years! Complete instructions for this program follow (page 42).

## A Reading Genealogy

- paternal grandfather
  - favorite childhood book
- paternal grandmother
  - favorite childhood book
- maternal grandfather
  - favorite childhood book
- maternal grandmother
  - favorite childhood book
- father
  - favorite childhood book
- mother
  - favorite childhood book
- my name
  - my favorite book

Name _____

# More Family Favorites

Book Title

## Aunts
_____
_____
_____
_____
_____

## Uncles
_____
_____
_____
_____
_____

## Others
_____
_____
_____
_____
_____

Name _____

**Awarded to** _____

for tracing a Reading Genealogy and reading _____ *Family Favorites!*

Date _____   Teacher/Librarian _____

*Family Favorites Reading Record*

Title

Recommended by

©1993 by Incentive Publications, Inc., Nashville, TN.

41

# A Reader's Time Capsule

Use this idea to plan for readers of tomorrow—and to stretch the imaginations and book-sharing capacities of readers of today! Explain to the children that, except for a few books that become classics, such as *Tom Sawyer* or *Heidi*, most books loved by one generation become forgotten in the next. Ask your class which of their book favorites they definitely don't want to be forgotten. Help your students create a time capsule that will persuade students of a later generation to read the books they love. When the capsule is finished, have the school library store it with a note attached giving readers of another generation the date it may be opened (10 years? 20 years?). This could become an annual event to be enjoyed by the makers and the openers for years to come!

## SUGGESTIONS FOR THE TIME CAPSULE

- Letters from students in the class telling about their favorite books and themselves. Attach a picture of the student to each letter.
- Have students talk about their favorite books on videotape. Put a videotape in the time capsule.
- Take a class vote to choose a book to be "overall favorite." Put in one or two paperback copies of the book.
- Have students design ads or commercials "selling" future students on trying the old favorites.
- Have students write short essays in which they imagine how books will be different for later readers, or which subjects later readers will enjoy.
- Give each student a "reminder slip" noting when the capsule will be opened and ask the student to put it in a safe place. The students may want to check back with the school and see how their "Reader's Time Capsule" was enjoyed!

## Future Sharing Form

Attach student photo here.

To readers of the year _____.
From: _____
____ age ____ grade ____

My favorite book is _____ by _____. I hope it won't be a forgotten book in the year _____. The best part of the book is:
_____
_____
_____
_____
_____

Date: _____

a bookmark "reminder" to save...

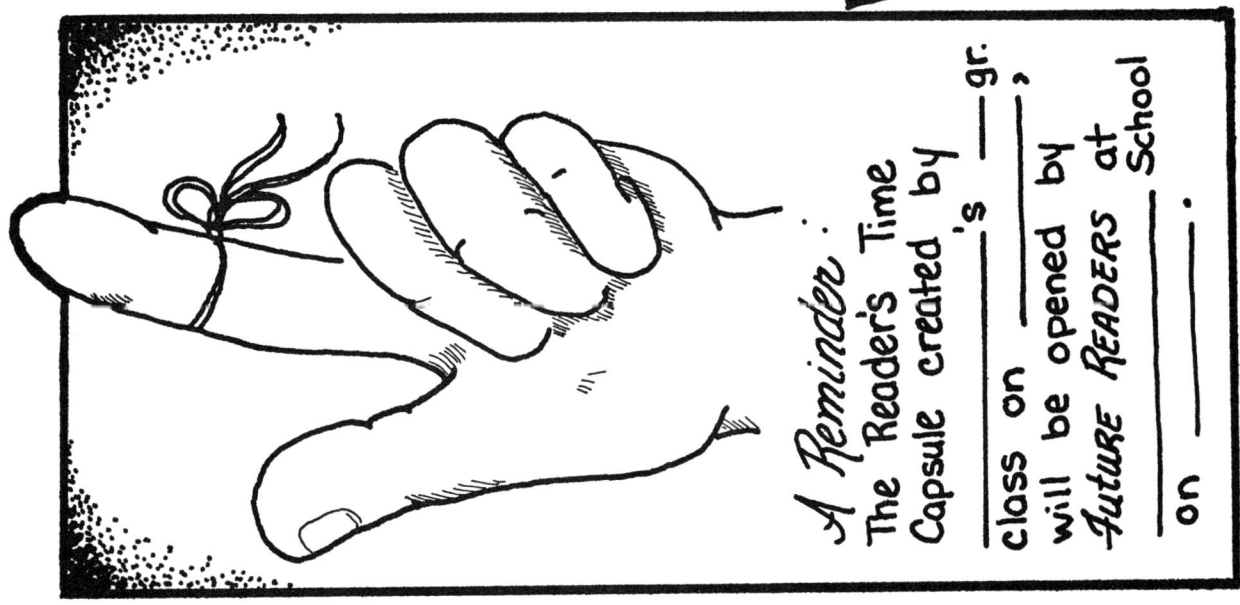

## A Reminder
The Reader's Time Capsule created by _____'s gr. ____ class on _____ will be opened by FUTURE READERS at _____ School on _____.

# BREAK FOR the BOOKS DAY!

Everyone gets tired of the same old boredom of daily routine. Beat the blahs and steer clear of textbooks with a "Break For The Books" Day! Structure your entire day around pleasure reading and literature-related activities!

## Here's how:

**1** **Announce your "Break For The Books Day" to students.** Encourage them to bring mats and pillows for comfort and loads of reading material to enjoy: newspapers, library books, magazines, even comic books!

**2** **Plan your day.** One way to avoid chaos and provide some structure is to design five or six different sessions and designate areas of the classroom for each session. Divide your students into groups of five. These groups will rotate together throughout the day. Color-code each of the designated areas of your classroom. For example, a red sign in one area might be labeled "Pleasure Reading Corner." In another area, a blue sign might announce "The Poetry Place," and so forth. Using the teacher's planner (page 50), decide which students to group together and which session they

BREAK FOR THE BOOKS DAY!
page 2

will attend at what time. Then prepare for each student a badge as shown. The colored stickers at the bottom of the badge will show the order in which the student will rotate. For example, if the first colored sticker is yellow, the student will know to attend the session marked by the yellow sign. He or she will know to move to the next color when the "time's up" signal is given.

*Use color-coded badges to help organize students for the day's activities*

## PLANNING SESSIONS

Plan the various sessions carefully, but try to keep each one simple. In each section, place a poster that explains what students are expected to do. You may circulate quietly among groups to make sure students understand what is expected. Have all necessary materials waiting in each designated area.

Some ideas for the designated areas are:

**A. Pleasure Reading corner:** This area is for students to enjoy silent reading of whatever material they choose: library books, comic books, magazines, etc.

**B. Tell Me a Story area:** Have listening stations set up with cassette players, headphones, and stories on cassette tape.

**C. Scavenger Hunt section:** Check out a selection of books from the library and send the students on a literature scavenger hunt in this area. You may choose to use the "Who Dun It" quiz (page 18). Duplicate a copy of the quiz for each group and display the books listed on page 19. The group may work quietly together to find as many answers as they can in the time allotted.

**D. Arts and Crafts section:** Arrange paper, markers, scissors, etc., on a table. Any number of ideas could be planned for this area. Some are:

- Have each student make a bookmark.

- Have each student make a cover for a book.

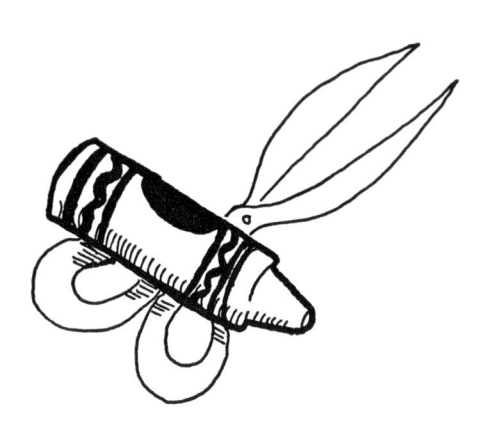

- Furnish a list of authors' birthdays, and a selection of books by each author. Each student can make a birthday card for a selected author, put it in an envelope, and address it to the author, in care of the publisher (information found on the title page). If you furnish wrapping paper in your center, students can giftwrap a book by the author and put a note on the top, "To be opened in March," for example. Keep these "gifts" and open the books to read to your class during the author's birth month.

- Have students make valentines or Christmas cards for favorite authors, illustrators, or book characters.

- Have each student design a comic strip based on his or her favorite book character.

**E. The Poetry Place:** Furnish lots of "fun" poetry books like Ciardi's *I Met A Man*, Viorst's *If I Were in Charge of the World*, and Silverstein's *The Light in the Attic* or *Where the Sidewalk Ends*. (Ask your librarian for other ideas.)

Have students choose a favorite poem and copy it for a classroom poetry file or booklet. It is not a good idea to ask students to write poetry unless you have already shared a good deal of poetry in the classroom, instilled a good feeling toward it, and practiced writing some, but if your students have already experienced this foundation for enjoyment, post the formulas for "non-threatening" poems like cinquains and diamantes. Furnish "neat" writing supplies: colored paper, pens, etc., and allow students to create some original poems for a book your class will "publish."

**Cinquain Formula**

Line 1: One word for the title

Line 2: Two words describing the title

Line 3: Three action words relating to the title

Line 4: Four words expressing a feeling about the title

Line 5: Another word repeating or similar to the title

**Cinquain Example:**
*Spaghetti*
*Hot, Delicious*
*Steaming, Oozing, Dripping*
*Good before a ballgame*
*Pasta*

**Diamante Formula**

Line 1: One noun

Line 2: Two adjectives describing the noun

Line 3: Three words expressing action relating to the noun

Line 4: Four nouns or a phrase showing a contrast between the noun and its opposite

Line 5: Three action words relating to the opposite

Line 6: Two adjectives describing the opposite

Line 7: Opposite noun

**Diamante Example:**
*Day*
*Bright, Light*
*Refreshing, Enlivening, Glistening*
*Light somehow goes away*
*Darkening, Whispering, Softening*
*Deep, Quiet*
*Night*

BREAK FOR THE BOOKS DAY!
page 5

**3** **Make your day go smoothly.** Explain color-coding to the students at the beginning of the day. To avoid chaos, designate one member of each team "captain." He or she may approach your desk when the group has a question. Arrange a signal so that the class will know when it is time to switch areas. For example, a bell rung once means to straighten the area, put away materials. A bell rung twice means to go on to the next color-coded area. A bell rung three times means to gather together in an entire group.

Intersperse the activities of the day with literature-related activities. Use the games described in this book: *Storybook Beano* (page 64), *The Name Game* (page 60), or *I'm a Bookworm* (page 61).

At the end of the day, give awards to teams for: The Quietest Group, The Most Responsible Group, The Group Winning the Literature Scavenger Hunt, etc.

You may choose to reward team members with Book Bucks (page 53)!

*Note:* Children generally understand that this is a special Quiet Day. You can set a "quiet" mood with your comments and preparations. (Be sure to hang the "Quiet: Readers in Residence" sign on the outside of your door!) First-timers may choose to ask a parent volunteer to spend the day with the class.

YOU MAY CHOOSE TO GIVE EACH GROUP A COLOR-CODED FOLDER INSTEAD OF A BADGE.

INSIDE THE GROUP CAN KEEP A RECORD OF THEIR DAY'S ACTIVITIES:
- ANSWERS TO SCAVENGER HUNT
- POETRY
- RECORD OF SILENT READING BY EACH STUDENT
- ETC.

THE TEACHER CAN MARK THE OUTSIDE OF THE FOLDER AFTER EACH SESSION WITH A "MARK FOR MERITOUS CONDUCT" AND REWARD GROUPS AT THE END OF THE DAY.

*Set the Mood* in your classroom with this DOORKNOB DECORATION

QUIET!

READERS in residence

*Run off copies for students to put on the doors of their rooms at home when they are reading.

©1993 by Incentive Publications, Inc., Nashville, TN.

# *Break For The Books!*
## Teacher's Planner

| Time | Color Code | Activity | Gr. # | Group Members |
|------|------------|----------|-------|---------------|
|      |            |          |       |               |
|      |            |          |       |               |
|      |            |          |       |               |
|      |            |          |       |               |
|      |            |          |       |               |

# THE BOOK BUCK INCENTIVE!

You won't be "passing the buck" with this winning idea! Reproduce a quantity of "book bucks" for your classroom. Use colored copying paper and use the master furnished for you on page 53 for easy reproduction. Use "book bucks" as rewards AND motivators! You may choose to use them in lieu of oft-used awards for academic or behavioral performance. Or you may choose to use them to reward performance in reading or book-sharing. However they are used, Book Bucks turn right around and work for you again . . . as MOTIVATORS! You are limited *only* by the limits of your own creativity!

## SOME BOOK BUCK SUGGESTIONS

- Use book bucks as passes for free reading time.
- Use book bucks as passes to the library during spare time.
- Occasionally let a student "pass the buck" on homework and use seatwork time as reading time.
- Work with local businesses and let book bucks earned for reading become free passes to the skating rink, passes for free movie rental (of movies based on books, preferably), free passes for a burger and fries, etc.
- Ask your librarian to schedule a movie based on a book and let book bucks buy the tickets . . . or do this in your own classroom, with book bucks paying for pop and popcorn, too! Tie it into a lesson on economics!

# THE BOOK BUCK INCENTIVE!
## page 2

### MORE BOOK BUCK IDEAS

- Let book bucks earn the privilege of decorating your bulletin boards.

- Let book bucks earn the privilege of working quietly with a group planning a puppet show or play for the class. (The show or play should be based on a book, of course!)

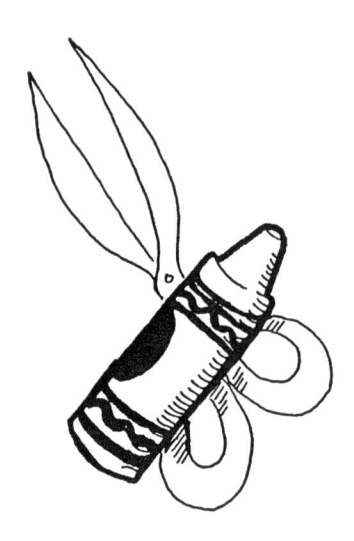

- Set up a "mini-store" in your classroom. Ask area businesses for small donations: erasers, pencils, advertising items (keychains, rulers, etc.). Let students buy items with the book bucks they have earned.

- Ask your librarian for worn books without covers. Set up a table in your classroom with markers, butcher paper, etc. Let book bucks earn a student the privilege of working quietly at the table to make attractive new covers for old books.

- Let book bucks become tickets for a field trip to the public library.

- Have fun! Creativity is the key to making this a success!

*Note:* Don't forget to set up your own economics system. Make a chart listing how many book bucks are earned for what and how many book bucks it takes to earn what. This will keep students from being confused and will motivate them still further. Also, it helps to have students sign the back of a book buck as they receive it so there's no mix-up concerning to whom it belongs. This helps the teacher, too: as the book bucks are returned in exchange for privileges, it is easy for the teacher to keep up with the degree of program involvement of individual students.

⇐ Reproduce and cut apart.

Use as rewards for book-activities and as motivators for special privileges.

©1993 by Incentive Publications, Inc., Nashville, TN.

53

## Door Decor:

# KNOCK, KNOCK! ON MY DOOR!

What child can resist a knock-knock joke? "Knock, Knock, On My Door" is a simple door decor idea intended to lure students to the 800's section of the library (where joke and riddle books are found), focus students on reading and fun, and give *you* an attractive display! Patterns for the witch, Hansel and Gretel, and the gingerbread houses are included in this section, along with a list of suggested "knock-knocks." But feel free to have fun and create your own!

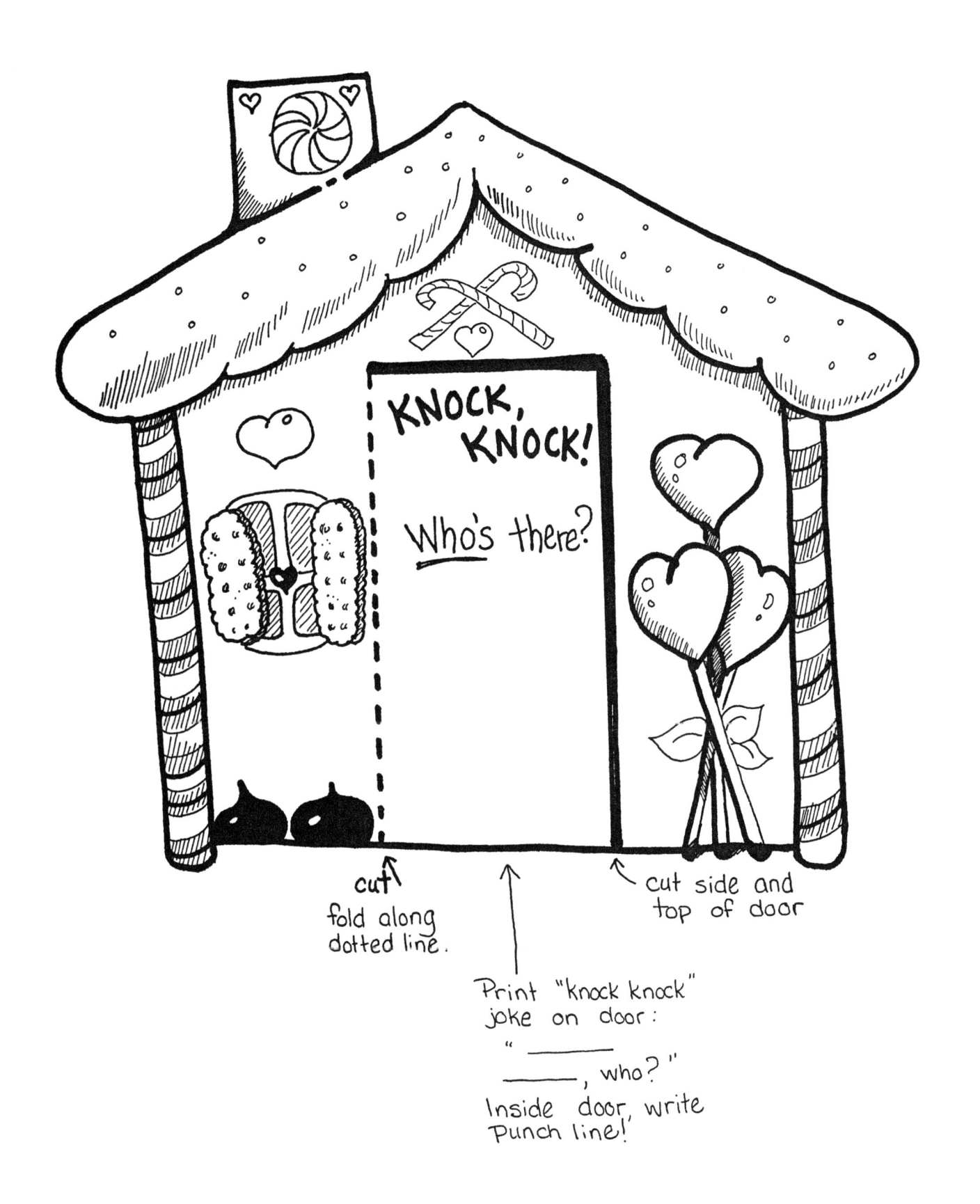

**KNOCK, KNOCK!**

**Who's there?**

cut
fold along dotted line.

cut side and top of door

Print "knock knock" joke on door:

" _____

_____, who?"

Inside door, write punch line!

©1993 by Incentive Publications, Inc., Nashville, TN.

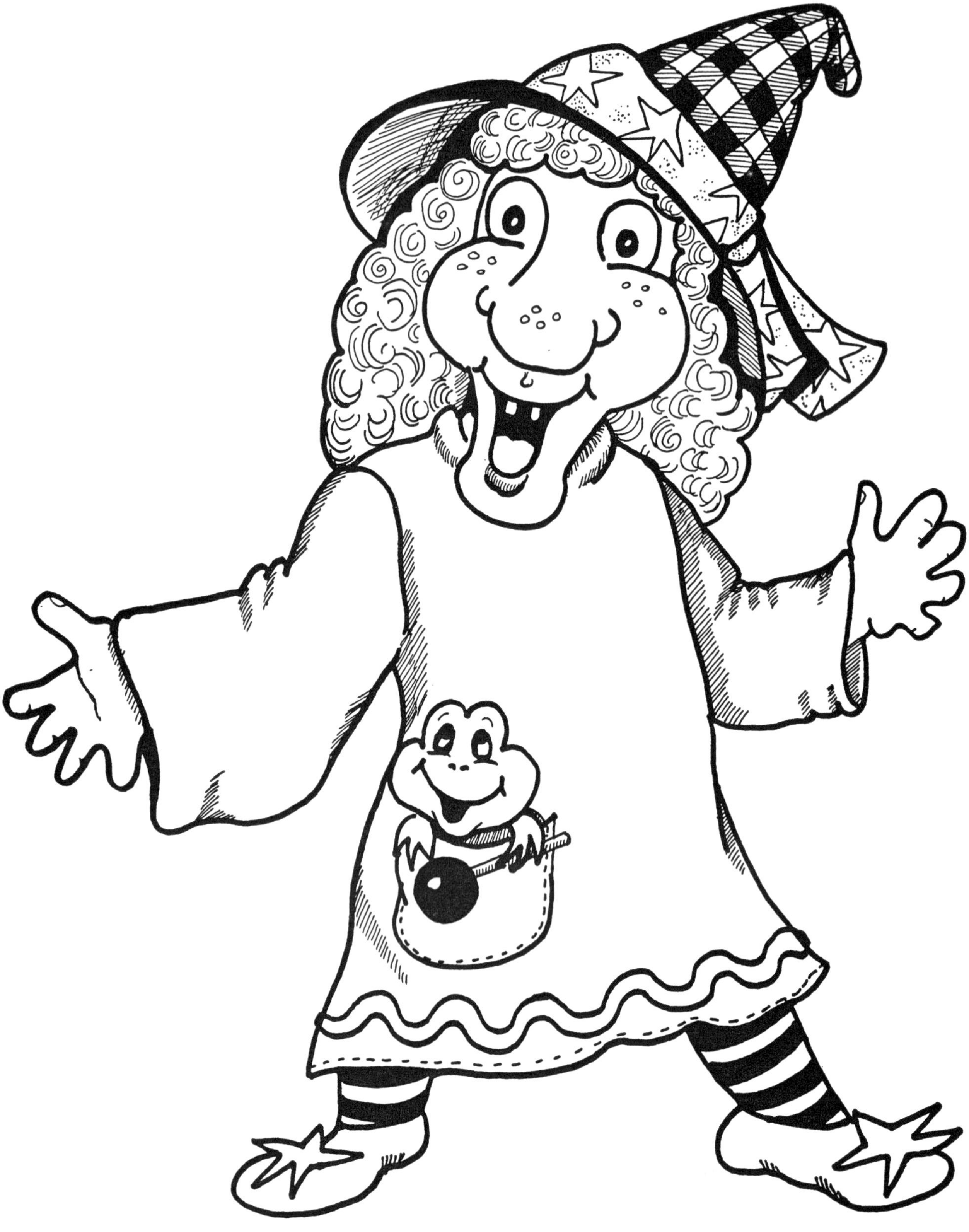

©1993 by Incentive Publications, Inc., Nashville, TN.

# KNOCK, KNOCK JOKES to use!

KNOCK! KNOCK!
Who's there?
EWELL.
Ewell who?
EWELL FIND KNOCK-KNOCK JOKES IN THE 800'S!

---

KNOCK! KNOCK!
Who's there?
RED.
Red who?
RED ANY GOOD BOOKS LATELY?

---

KNOCK! KNOCK!
Who's there?
RITA.
Rita who?
RITA BOOK A DAY!

---

KNOCK! KNOCK!
Who's there?
CONSUMPTION.
Consumption who?
CONSUMPTION BE DONE ABOUT YOUR KNOCKING ON MY DOOR?

---

KNOCK! KNOCK!
Who's there?
BAT.
Bat who?
BAT YOU JUST LOVE JOKE AND RIDDLE BOOKS!

---

KNOCK! KNOCK!
Who's there?
DEWEY.
Dewey who?
DEWEY HAVE JOKE BOOKS IN THE LIBRARY?

---

KNOCK! KNOCK!
Who's there?
WITCH.
Witch who?
WITCH OF YOU IS BOTHERING ME THIS TIME?

---

KNOCK! KNOCK!
Who's there?
WANDA.
Wanda who?
WANDA COME IN AND LISTEN TO A STORY?

# GAMES READERS PLAY

# THE NAME GAME

Reinforce children's knowledge of book and traditional literature characters with this guessing game! Here's how:

1. Make a quantity of cards with male and female book characters' names printed on them. Some suggestions are: Cinderella, Snow White, the Beast (of *Beauty and the Beast*), Henry Huggins, Ramona, Little Arlis (of *Old Yeller*), Mike Mulligan, Frances, Corduroy, etc.
2. Attach yarn long enough to fit over a child's head as shown below.
3. Choose a volunteer to be a character.
4. Show the class the name on the card, but do not show it to the volunteer. Fit it over his or her neck so it hangs on his or her back.
5. The volunteer asks the class questions to determine which character he or she is supposed to be. Questions should be general at first: "Am I male or female?" "Am I a person or an animal?" Questions will become more specific as the volunteer narrows down options: "Am I in a fairy tale?" "Am I in the book _____?" All questions must be the kind that can be answered with "yes" or "no."

*Note:* This is an activity children love, but teachers may have to aid in prompting questions until students get the knack of what kinds of questions to ask.

*I'M A BOOKWORM AND I'VE READ Charlotte's Web, Sounder, Blubber, A Chair for my Mother, Miss Nelson is missing, Harriet the Spy, Where the Red Fern Grows...*

# I'm A Bookworm...

Have fun, familiarize students with book titles, and reinforce those cognitive skills, all with the same activity! "I'm a Bookworm" is a take-off on the old familiar "I went to the grocery store..."

Here's how to play:

- Choose a student to begin, "I'm a bookworm and I've read _____ (any title)."

- The next student will repeat, "I'm a bookworm and I've read _____ (first student's title) and _____ (new title)."

- Play will continue around the room with each student repeating what has been said previously and adding a new title.

- As students begin to forget the order, they drop out of play. The last student to remain in the game wins.

*Hint:* This game is a great filler when there is spare time, or a good culminating activity at the end of a school day. You might want to reproduce a Book Buck (page 53) for the winner!

# "Shake" out the CHARACTERS!

"Shake Out the Characters" is a variation of the old familiar game "Upset the Fruit Basket." It is a good activity to use for P.E., rainy days, story hours, Literature Celebration parties, or any time you want students to have some active fun while keeping the focus on books!

Students are seated in chairs arranged in a circle. The teacher assigns a character name to each student, from one of several categories: Fairy Tale Characters, Tall Tale Characters, Picture Book People, Storybook Animals, etc. (A suggested list is provided for you on the following page.) When the teacher calls out a category, those characters in the category will all jump up and try to find another chair. (For example, when the teacher says "Shake out the Fairy Tale characters!" Snow White, the Frog Prince, Cinderella, and Rapunzel will jump up.) Of course, the teacher will remove one chair from the circle as soon as the students jump up! Play continues with students never knowing which category might be called, until only one character is left.

The neatest thing about this game is that students are learning genres and classification of characters while they have active fun. Of course, after being "Johnny Appleseed" for 15 or so minutes, a student may decide he wants to read about him!

# Suggested Lists For "Shake Out The Characters!"

## FAIRY TALE CHARACTERS

- Prince Charming
- Snow White
- Sleeping Beauty
- The Frog Prince
- Cinderella
- Fairy Godmother
- Hansel
- Gretel
- Rapunzel
- Rose Red
- Briar Rose

## MOTHER GOOSE CHARACTERS

- Little Boy Blue
- Jack Sprat
- Miss Muffet
- Little Tommy Tucker
- Little Bo Peep
- Old King Cole
- Mistress Mary
- Tom, the Piper's Son
- Little Jack Horner

## TALL TALE CHARACTERS

- John Henry
- Johnny Appleseed
- Pecos Bill
- Sluefoot Sue
- Paul Bunyan
- Joe Magarac
- Febold Feboldsen
- Davy Crockett

## PICTURE BOOK PEOPLE

- Amelia Bedelia
- Everett Anderson
- Little Sal
- Bartholomew Cubbins
- Alexander
- Mike Mulligan
- Strega Nona
- Drummer Hoff
- Max

## STORYBOOK ANIMALS

- Curious George
- Wilbur
- Charlotte
- Peter Rabbit
- The Cat in the Hat
- Petunia
- Frances
- Sylvester
- Chester Chipmunk

# STORYBOOK BEANO!

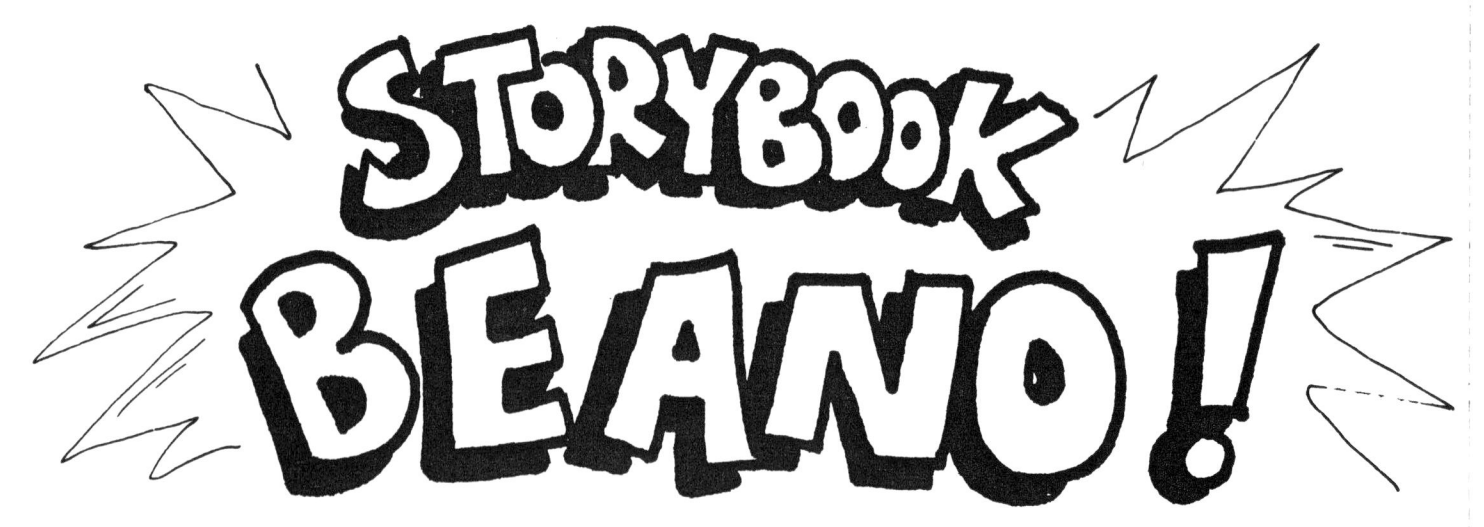

I first created Storybook Beano over twenty years ago when I began working as a children's aide in a public library. Although it was first intended primarily as a filler activity, I soon became amazed at the amount of book-sharing and impromptu book talks that resulted from it. Call out a title a child loves and he or she just can't resist! You'll find Storybook Beano great book bait!

You are given the materials to create either a primary or intermediate Storybook Beano set. Here's how:

1. Reproduce the blank Storybook Beano Answer Card (page 78) in a quantity sufficient for your class.

2. Choose either the Primary or Intermediate Call Card set (pages 69-71 or pages 75-77). Laminate and cut apart the Call Cards.

3. Using the primary Title Listing (pages 66-68) or the intermediate Title Listing (pages 72-74) as your resource, begin filling in the spaces on the Answer Cards. Ask students to help. Although complete bibliographic information is given in the Title Listings, write only the title of a book in a space. Write only those titles listed under B on the answer cards under B, those listed under E on the answer cards under E, and so forth. Twenty titles are listed under each letter, and there are only five blocks under the same letter on the answer card (except for E, which has a "free beano"), so if you mix up titles at random as you fill in the spaces, odds of getting a card with exactly the same titles are not great. You would be wise to laminate the answer cards when you are finished filling them in to ensure that they can be used again year after year.

Teachers with large classes will be grateful to discover that much of the writing by hand can be avoided by reproducing the Call Card pages and cutting the rectangles apart to be pasted onto the Answer Cards. You will find that the Call Cards are positioned so that many of them can be pasted onto the Answer Cards in strips. You will need to paste down individual rectangles in order to use the rectangles printed on the right-hand sides of the pages or if it becomes necessary to do so in order to make sure each Answer Card is different from the others.

STORYBOOK BEANO!
*page 2*

4. Fill reclosable sandwich bags with a handful of beans. The beans will serve as markers. (A simple warning, "Beans in the floor, we play no more!" will take care of any bean-spilling mischief—children love to play this game!)

*Note:* Although master lists are given to you in this book, there is no reason you can't use the blank answer cards and create your own Reading Beano. You may choose to make a Caldecott, Newbery, Reading Rainbow, or Classroom Favorites Beano game.

## PLAYING RULES

The rules of Storybook Beano are exactly the same as those for regular "Bingo." Drawing a card from the pile of Call Cards, the teacher calls out a letter and a title. Example: *B, Charlotte's Web*. The student looks under the letter B on his or her Answer Card. If the title is written in one of the squares, the student places a bean on it. A row of beans straight across, straight down, or running diagonally from corner to corner wins the game. Give a treat, a bookmark, or a Book Buck for a prize.

… STORYBOOK BEANO!

# PRIMARY TITLE LISTING

# B

**Charlie Needs a Cloak,** Tomie de Paola. Prentice Hall.
**How the Grinch Stole Christmas,** Dr. Seuss. Random House.
**I'll Fix Anthony,** Judith Viorst. Atheneum.
**Everett Anderson's Nine Month Long,** Lucille Clifton. Holt, Rinehart and Winston.
**Don't Forget the Bacon,** Pat Hutchins. Morrow.
**Arthur's Eyes,** Marc Brown. Avon Books.
**Apple Tree Christmas,** Trinka Hakes Noble. Dial.
**Abiyoyo,** Pete Seeger. MacMillan.
**Adventures of Albert the Running Bear,** Barbara Isenberg and Susan Wolf. Houghton Mifflin.
**The Caterpillar and the Polliwog,** Jack Kent. Simon and Schuster.
**Cherries and Cherry Pits,** Vera Williams. Morrow.
**Hey, Al,** Arthur Yorinks. Farrar, Straus, Giroux.
**Journey Cake, Ho!** Ruth Sawyer. Viking Penguin.
**Louis the Fish,** Arthur Yorinks. Farrar, Straus, Giroux.
**Miss Nelson is Missing,** Harry Allard. Scholastic Book Service.
**Mousekin's Golden House,** Edna Miller. Prentice Hall.
**Mushroom in the Rain,** Mirra Ginsburg. Aladdin.
**Pumpkin Moonshine,** Tasha Tudor. Random House.
**The Talking Eggs,** Robert D. San Souci. Dial.
**Flossie and the Fox,** Patricia C. McKissack. Dial.

# STORYBOOK BEANO!

# E

Horton Hears a Who!, Dr. Seuss. Random House.
Gregory, the Terrible Eater, Mitchell Sharmat. Four Winds.
Caps for Sale, Esphyr Slobodkina. Young Scott Books.
Sylvester and the Magic Pebble, William Steig. Simon and Schuster.
Anatole, Eve Titus. McGraw-Hill.
A Tree is Nice, Janice Udry. Harper and Row.
Crictor, Tomi Ungerer. Harper and Row.
Polar Express, Chris Van Allsburg. Houghton Mifflin.
The Tenth Good Thing About Barney, Judith Viorst. Atheneum.
The Biggest Bear, Lynd Ward. Houghton Mifflin.

A Chair for my Mother, Vera B. Williams. Greenwillow.
The Napping House, Audrey Wood. HBJ.
Anansi the Spider, Gerald McDermott. Holt, Rinehart, Winston.
Amelia Bedelia, Peggy Parrish. Harper and Row.
Cranberry Halloween, Wende and Harry Devlin. Aladdin.
Time of Wonder, Robert McCloskey. Viking.
The Funny Little Woman, Arlene Mosel. Dutton.
Lon Po Po: a Red Riding Hood Story from China, Ed Young. Putnam.
Noah's Ark, Peter Spier. Doubleday.
Little Red Hen, Paul Galdone. Houghton Mifflin.

# A

King Bidgood's in the Bathtub, Audrey Wood. HBJ.
One Fine Day, Nonny Hogrogrian. MacMillan Co.
Once A Mouse, Marcia Brown. Atheneum.
Snow White and the Seven Dwarfs, Grimm and Burkert. Farrar, Straus, Giroux.
The Snowy Day, Ezra Jack Keats. Viking Penguin.
Wagon Wheels, Barbara Brenner. Harper and Row.
When I Was Young in the Mountains, Cynthia Rylant. Dutton.
Hailstones and Halibut Bones, Mary O'Neill. Doubleday.
Fox in Socks, Dr. Seuss. Random House.
The Fox Went Out on a Chilly Night, Peter Spier. Doubleday.

Clifford the Big Red Dog, Norman Bridwell. Scholastic Book Service.
Abraham Lincoln, Ingri and Edgar D'Aulaire. Doubleday.
Adventures of Obadiah, Brinton Turkle. Viking Penguin.
Alexander and the Terrible, Horrible, No-Good, Very Bad Day, Judith Viorst. Atheneum.
Anno's Journey, Mitsumasa Anno. G.P. Putnam.
Applebet: An ABC, Wendy and Clyde Watson. Farrar, Straus, Giroux.
Ask Mr. Bear, Marjorie Flack. MacMillan.
Baba Yaga, Ernest Small. Houghton Mifflin.
Babar the King, Jean de Brunhoff. Knopf.
The Baby Uggs are Hatching, Jack Prelutsky. Morrow.

# N

**Blackboard Bear,** Martha Alexander. Dial.

**Ape in a Cape,** Fritz Eichenberg. HBJ.

**Humbug Witch,** Lorna Balian. Abingdon.

**The Easter Egg Artists,** Adrienne Adams. Scribner.

**The Runaway Bunny,** Margaret W. Brown. Harper and Row.

**Daniel's Duck,** Clyde R. Bulla. Harper and Row.

**Mike Mulligan and His Steam Shovel,** Virginia L. Burton. Houghton Mifflin.

**The Very Hungry Caterpillar,** Eric Carle. Philomel.

**Hot-Air Henry,** Mary Calhoun. Morrow.

**Miss Rumphius,** Barbara Cooney. Viking.

**Strega Nona,** Tomie de Paola. Prentice Hall.

**Ox-Cart Man,** Donald Hall. Viking.

**The Big Snow,** Elmer and Berta Hader. MacMillan.

**Ben's Trumpet,** Rachel Isadora. Greenwillow.

**Round Trip,** Ann Jones. Greenwillow.

**The Snowy Day,** Ezra Jack Keats. Viking.

**Swimmy,** Leo Lionni. Pantheon.

**Frog and Toad Together,** Arnold Lobel. Harper and Row.

**Blueberries for Sal,** Robert McCloskey. Viking.

**The Hundred Penny Box,** Sharon Mathis. Viking.

# O

**Goodnight Moon,** Margaret W. Brown. Harper and Row.

**Nana Upstairs and Nana Downstairs,** Tomie de Paola. Putnam.

**Nine Days to Christmas,** Marie Hall Ets. Viking.

**Corduroy,** Don Freeman. Viking.

**Millions of Cats,** Wanda Gag. Coward-McCann.

**Little Toot,** Hardie Gramatky. Putnam.

**Make Way for Ducklings,** Robert McCloskey. Viking.

**There's a Nightmare in My Closet,** Mercer Mayer. Dial.

**The Drinking Gourd,** F. N. Monjo. Harper and Row.

**Little Bear,** Else H. Minarik. Harper and Row.

**Song of the Swallows,** Leo Politi. Scribner.

**The Tale of Squirrel Nutkin,** Beatrix Potter. Warne.

**Curious George,** H. A. Rey. Houghton Mifflin.

**The Relatives Came,** Cynthia Rylant. Bradbury.

**Rain Makes Applesauce,** Julian Scheer. Holiday House.

**Where the Wild Things Are,** Maurice Sendak. Harper and Row.

**Green Eggs and Ham,** Dr. Seuss. Beginner Book.

**Heckedy Peg,** Audrey Wood. HB.

**The Z was Zapped,** Chris Van Allsburg. Houghton Mifflin.

**Digging Up Dinosaurs,** Aliki. Harper and Row.

# PRIMARY CALL CARDS

STORYBOOK BEANO!

| B | E | A | N | O | B |
|---|---|---|---|---|---|
| Charlie Needs A Cloak | Horton Hears a Who! | King Bidgood's in the Bathtub | Blackboard Bear | Goodnight Moon | The Talking Eggs |

| B | E | A | N | O | E |
|---|---|---|---|---|---|
| How The Grinch Stole Christmas | Gregory, the Terrible Eater | One Fine Day | Ape in a Cape | Nana Upstairs and Nana Downstairs | Noah's Ark |

| B | E | A | N | O | A |
|---|---|---|---|---|---|
| I'll Fix Anthony | Caps for Sale | Once a Mouse | Humbug Witch | Nine Days to Christmas | Babar the King |

| B | E | A | N | O | N |
|---|---|---|---|---|---|
| Everett Anderson's Nine Month Long | Sylvester and the Magic Pebble | Snow White and the Seven Dwarfs | The Easter Egg Artists | Corduroy | Blueberries for Sal |

| B | E | A | N | O | O |
|---|---|---|---|---|---|
| Don't Forget the Bacon | Anatole | The Snowy Day | The Runaway Bunny | Millions of Cats | The Z was Zapped |

| B | E | A | N | O |
|---|---|---|---|---|
| Arthur's Eyes | A Tree is Nice | Wagon Wheels | Daniel's Duck | Little Toot |

©1993 by Incentive Publications, Inc., Nashville, TN.

# PRIMARY CALL CARDS

STORYBOOK BEANO!

| B | E | A | N | O | B |
|---|---|---|---|---|---|
| Apple Tree Christmas | Crictor | When I Was Young in the Mountains | Mike Mulligan and his Steam Shovel | Make Way for Ducklings | Flossie and the Fox |
| **B** Abiyoyo | **E** The Polar Express | **A** Hailstones and Halibut Bones | **N** The Very Hungry Caterpillar | **O** There's A Nightmare in My Closet | **E** Little Red Hen |
| **B** Adventures of Albert the Running Bear | **E** The Tenth Good Thing About Barney | **A** Fox in Socks | **N** Hot-Air Henry | **O** The Drinking Gourd | **A** The Baby Uggs are Hatching |
| **B** The Caterpillar and the Polliwog | **E** The Biggest Bear | **A** The Fox Went Out on a Chilly Night | **N** Miss Rumphius | **O** Little Bear | **N** The Hundred Penny Box |
| **B** Cherries and Cherry Pits | **E** A Chair for My Mother | **A** Clifford and the Big Red Dog | **N** Strega Nona | **O** Song of the Swallows | **O** Digging Up Dinosaurs |
| **B** Hey, Al | **E** The Napping House | **A** Abraham Lincoln | **N** Ox-Cart Man | **O** The Tale of Squirrel Nutkin | |

©1993 by Incentive Publications, Inc., Nashville, TN.

70

# PRIMARY CALL CARDS

STORYBOOK BEANO!

| B | E | A | N | O |
|---|---|---|---|---|
| Journey Cake, Ho! | Anansi the Spider | Adventures of Obadiah | The Big Snow | Curious George |
| Louis the Fish | Amelia Bedelia | Alexander and the Terrible, Horrible, No Good, Very Bad Day | Ben's Trumpet | The Relatives Came |
| Miss Nelson is Missing | Cranberry Halloween | Anno's Journey | Round Trip | Rain Makes Applesauce |
| Mousekin's Golden House | Time of Wonder | Applebet | The Snowy Day | Where the Wild Things Are |
| Mushroom in the Rain | The Funny Little Woman | Ask Mr. Bear | Swimmy | Green Eggs and Ham |
| Pumpkin Moonshine | Lon Po Po | Baba Yaga | Frog and Toad Together | Heckedy Peg |

©1993 by Incentive Publications, Inc., Nashville, TN.

STORYBOOK BEANO!

# INTERMEDIATE TITLE LISTING

# B

**Blubber,** Judy Blume. Dell.
**Caddie Woodlawn,** Carol Brink. MacMillan.
**Ginger Pye,** Eleanor Estes. Harcourt, Brace, Jovanovich.
**The Indian in the Cupboard,** Lynn Banks. Avon.
**Old Yeller,** Fred Gipson. Harper and Row.
**4B Goes Wild,** Jamie Gilson. Lothrop, Lee, & Shepherd.
**Bedknob and Broomstick,** Mary Norton. Harcourt, Brace, Jovanovich.
**Island of the Blue Dolphins,** Scott O'Dell. Houghton Mifflin.
**Where the Red Fern Grows,** Wilson Rawls. Doubleday.
**Freaky Friday,** Mary Rodgers. Harper and Row.
**The First Hard Times,** Doris Buchanan Smith. Viking.
**Mary Poppins,** P. L. Travers. Harcourt, Brace, Jovanovich.
**Jumanji,** Chris Van Allsburg. Houghton Mifflin.
**Charlotte's Web,** E.B. White. Harper and Row.
**J.T.,** Jane Wagner. Dell.
**The Dollhouse Murders,** Betty Wright. Holiday House.
**Dragonwings,** Laurence Yep. Harper and Row.
**Sing Down the Moon,** Scott O'Dell. Dell.
**The Whipping Boy,** Sid Fleischman. Morrow.
**Just So Stories,** Rudyard Kipling. New American Library.

# E

Charlie and the Chocolate Factory, Roald Dahl. Bantam.
Land That I Lost, Q. Huynh. Harper and Row.
Anpao: An American Indian Odyssey, J. Highwater. Harper and Row.
The Headless Cupid, Zilpha Keatley. Snyder, Atheneum.
Homesick, Jean Fritz. Dell Yearling.
Lincoln, Russell Freedman. Houghton Mifflin.
Twenty-One Balloons, William Pene Dubois. Dell.
Lion Hound, James Kjelgaard. Bantam.
Sugaring Time, Kathryn Lasky. Atheneum.
The Moves Make the Man, Bruce Brooks. Harper and Row.
The Kid in the Red Jacket, Barbara Park. Knopf.
The Light in the Attic, Shel Silverstein. Harper and Row.
The Matchlock Gun, Walter Edmonds. Troll.
Adventures of Tom Sawyer, Mark Twain. New American Library.
Akarak, James Houston. Harcourt, Brace Jovanovich.
Calico Captive, Elizabeth Speare. Dell Yearling.
Sarah, Plain and Tall, Patricia MacLachlan. Harper and Row.
Just As Long As We're Together, Judy Blume. MacMillan.
M. C. Higgins the Great, Virginia Hamilton. MacMillan.
The Remembering Box, E. Clifford. Houghton Mifflin.

# A

You Come Too, Robert Frost. Holt, Rinehart, Wilson.
Maniac Magee, Jerry Spinelli. Little, Brown, & Co.
James and the Giant Peach, Roald Dahl. Viking.
The Jack Tales, Richard Chase. Houghton Mifflin.
The Hundred Penny Box, Sharon Bell Mathis. Viking.
Number the Stars, Lois Lowry, Dell Yearling.
Hatchet, Gary Paulsen, Viking.
Dicey's Song, Cynthia Voigt. Fawcett.
Come Sing, Jimmy Jo, Katherine Patterson. Avon.
The Cricket in Times Square, George Selden. Dell.
A Wrinkle in Time, Madeleine L'Engle. Dell Yearling.
Pyramid, David MacCauley. Houghton Mifflin.
Tuck Everlasting, Natalie Babbitt. Farrar, Straus, Giroux.
I Met a Man, John Ciardi. Houghton Mifflin.
Where the Sidewalk Ends, Shel Silverstein. Harper and Row.
The People Could Fly, Virginia Hamilton. Knopf.
Yeh Shen, Al Ling Louie. Putnam.
One-Eyed Cat, Paula Fox. Dell Yearling.
Ralph S. Mouse, Beverly Cleary. Dell.
The Witch of Blackbird Pond, Elizabeth Speare. Dell Yearling.

# STORYBOOK BEANO!

# N

Sounder, William Armstrong. Harper and Row.

Mr. Popper's Penguins, Richard Atwater. Little, Brown.

The Eyes of the Amaryllis, Natalie Babbit. Farrar, Straus, Giroux.

Miss Hickory, Carolyn S. Bailey. Viking.

The Wizard of Oz, Frank Baum. Grosset and Dunlap.

Freckle Juice, Judy Blume. Four Winds.

Superfudge, Judy Blume. Dutton.

The Pinballs, Betsy Byars. Harper and Row.

Dear Mr. Henshaw, Beverly Cleary. Morrow.

Harriet the Spy, Louise Fitzhugh. Harper and Row.

Old Yeller, Fred Gipson. Harper and Row.

Like Jake and Me, Mavis Jukes. Knopf.

Rabbit Hill, Robert Lawson. Viking.

The Lion, The Witch and the Wardrobe, C.S. Lewis. MacMillan.

Pippi Longstocking, Astrid Lindgren. Viking.

The Root Cellar, Janet Lunn. Scribner.

Gentle Ben, Walt Morey. Dutton.

The Borrowers, Mary Norton. HBJ.

Mrs. Frisby and the Rats of NIMH, Robert C. O'Brien. Atheneum.

Bridge to Terabithia, Katherine Paterson. Crowell.

# O

The Yearling, Marjorie Rawlings. Scribner.

The Best Christmas Pageant Ever, Barbara Robinson. Harper and Row.

How to Eat Fried Worms, Thomas Rockwell. Watts.

The Little Prince, Antoine de St.-Exupery. HBJ.

Black Beauty, Anna Sewell. SBS.

A Taste of Blackberries, Doris B. Smith. Crowell.

Encyclopedia Brown, Boy Detective, Donald Sobol. Bantam.

Abe Lincoln Grows Up, Carl Sandburg. HBJ.

Anastasia Krupnik, Lois Lowry. Houghton Mifflin.

The Boxcar Children, Gertrude Warner. Whitman.

Bridge to Terabithia, Katherine Paterson. Crowell.

Brighty of the Grand Canyon, Marguerite Henry. Checkerboard.

By the Shores of Silver Lake, Laura Ingalls Wilder. Harper and Row.

The Children of Greene Knowe, L.M. Boston. HBJ.

Christmas With Ida Early, Robert Burch. Viking.

Henry Huggins, Beverly Cleary. Morrow.

Where the Lilies Bloom, Vera Cleaver. Lippincott.

The House of Sixty Fathers, Meindert DeJong. Harper and Row.

Julie of the Wolves, Jean C. George. Harper and Row.

The Grandfather Tales, Richard Chase. Houghton Mifflin.

# INTERMEDIATE CALL CARDS

STORYBOOK BEANO!

| B | E | A | N | O | B |
|---|---|---|---|---|---|
| Blubber | Charlie & the Chocolate Factory | You Come Too | Sounder | The Yearling | The Whipping Boy |
| **B**<br>Caddie Woodlawn | **E**<br>Land That I Lost | **A**<br>Maniac Magee | **N**<br>Mr. Popper's Penguins | **O**<br>The Best Christmas Pageant Ever | **E**<br>M. C. Higgins, the Great |
| **B**<br>Ginger Pye | **E**<br>Anpao | **A**<br>James and the Giant Peach | **N**<br>The Eyes of the Amaryllis | **O**<br>How to Eat Fried Worms | **A**<br>Ralph S. Mouse |
| **B**<br>The Indian in the Cupboard | **E**<br>The Headless Cupid | **A**<br>The Jack Tales | **N**<br>Miss Hickory | **O**<br>The Little Prince | **N**<br>Mrs. Frisby and the Rats of NIMH |
| **B**<br>Old Yeller | **E**<br>Homesick | **A**<br>The Hundred Penny Box | **N**<br>The Wizard of Oz | **O**<br>Black Beauty | **O**<br>Julie of the Wolves |
| **B**<br>4B Goes Wild | **E**<br>Lincoln | **A**<br>Number the Stars | **N**<br>Freckle Juice | **O**<br>A Taste of Blackberries | |

©1993 by Incentive Publications, Inc., Nashville, TN.

# INTERMEDIATE CALL CARDS
STORYBOOK BEANO!

| B | E | A | N | O | B |
|---|---|---|---|---|---|
| Bedknob and Broomstick | Twenty-One Balloons | Hatchet | Superfudge | Encyclopedia Brown, Boy Detective | Just So Stories |
| **B** Island of the Blue Dolphins | **E** Lion Hound | **A** Dicey's Song | **N** The Pinballs | **O** Abe Lincoln Grows Up | **E** The Remembering Box |
| **B** Where the Red Fern Grows | **E** Sugaring Time | **A** Come Sing, Jimmy Jo | **N** Dear Mr. Henshaw | **O** Anastasia Krupnik | **A** The Witch of Blackbird Pond |
| **B** Freaky Friday | **E** The Moves Make the Man | **A** The Cricket in Times Square | **N** Harriet the Spy | **O** The Boxcar Children | **N** Bridge to Terabithia |
| **B** The First Hard Times | **E** The Kid in the Red Jacket | **A** A Wrinkle in Time | **N** Old Yeller | **O** Bridge To Terabithia | **O** The Grandfather Tales |
| **B** Mary Poppins | **E** The Light in the Attic | **A** Pyramid | **N** Like Jake and Me | **O** Brighty of the Grand Canyon | |

©1993 by Incentive Publications, Inc., Nashville, TN.

# INTERMEDIATE CALL CARDS
## STORYBOOK BEANO!

| B | E | A | N | O |
|---|---|---|---|---|
| Jumanji | The Matchlock Gun | Tuck Everlasting | Rabbit Hill | By the Shores of Silver Lake |
| Charlotte's Web | The Adventures of Tom Sawyer | I Met a Man | The Lion, the Witch, and the Wardrobe | The Children of Green Knowe |
| J. T. | Akarak | Where the Sidewalk Ends | Pippi Longstocking | Christmas with Ida Early |
| The Dollhouse Murders | Calico Captive | The People Could Fly | The Root Cellar | Henry Huggins |
| Dragonwings | Sarah, Plain and Tall | Yeh Shen | Gentle Ben | Where the Lilies Bloom |
| Sing Down the Moon | Just As Long As We're Together | One-Eyed Cat | The Borrowers | The House of Sixty Fathers |

©1993 by Incentive Publications, Inc., Nashville, TN.

Answer Card

# STORYBOOK BEANO

| B | E | A | N | O |
|---|---|---|---|---|
| B | E | A | N | O |
| B | E | (Paste-up handwritten FREE here) | N | O |
| B | E | A | N | O |
| B | E | A | N | O |

©1993 by Incentive Publications, Inc., Nashville, TN.

78

PROF
372.6
PH1